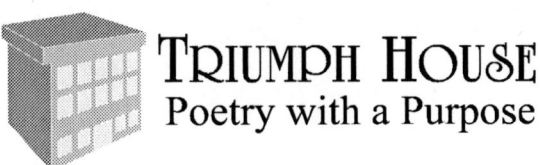

YOUNG & FOOLISH

Edited by

CHRIS WALTON

First published in Great Britain in 1998 by
TRIUMPH HOUSE
1-2 Wainman Road, Woodston,
Peterborough, PE2 7BU
Telephone (01733) 230749

All Rights Reserved

Copyright Contributors 1998

HB ISBN 1 86161 492 6
SB ISBN 1 86161 497 7

FOREWORD

We were all *Young and Foolish* at some point in our lives. In this anthology new and established poets celebrate these times and examine the way in which carefree moments have affected their adult lives.

Using one of the most expressive forms of the English language; poetry, these poets create humorous and anecdotal stories for readers to enjoy for years to come.

We believe this anthology will raise a smile or two, and spark forgotten memories from your own *Young and Foolish years*.

Chris Walton
Editor

CONTENTS

Full Circle	Patricia Battye	1
1973	Tracie Mark Deakin	2
Special Thoughts	Tara Kay	3
Nosy Parker	Ian T Colley	4
Recycled Pain	Beverley Christian	5
Anaesthesia	G Richardson	6
Days Gone By	Rose Schwarz	8
The Dance of Life	V B Aspinall	9
My Dad	Dorothy Fisher	10
To Be Young And Foolish	Stanislaw Paul Dabrowski-Oakland	11
Our Class Of 1952	M C Davies	12
Our Heartbeat	Dark Rose	13
Easter Monday	Barry Welburn	14
Time	Julie Coulborn	15
Young & Foolish	Joyce E Williams	16
Sweet Reigate	Frederica Morgan	17
Looking Back	Jean Kennedy	18
Young And Foolish	Gladys Lamb	19
Life's Springtime	Eileen N Blackmore	20
Fear	K V Land	21
The Awakening	Katy Melia	22
Wise Words	Steve Taylor	23
Mum And Dad	P A Deakin	24
A Memoir From A Budding Fag-Ash Lil	J Baker	25
My Night Of Rebellion	Victoria Joan Theedam	26
Funny Day	Hannah Jackson	27
Then And Now	Vera Homer	28
Memories	Ethel Grange	29
Eden	Eileen Pennell	30
Full-Up	Pam Phillips	31
Observations and Examples	A J Ogg	32
Mother's Milk	Peter Lee	33
To Be Young And Foolish	N Tomlinson	34
My Fairies	Charles H Boyett	35

Title	Author	Page
The Skateboard	Anita Jane Smith	36
Exam Results	Kimberley Forsyth	37
Frightening Enlightening	Gordon Haines	38
Adolescent Folly	Amanda-Lea Manning	39
Memories Of Christmas	K Hines	40
Changes In Farming	R J Moultan	41
Winter When . . .	A Humphrey	42
Not Rosy Tints	Graeme Vine	43
Young And Foolish	Francine	44
A Forgotten Language	Elizabeth Rae	45
Splish, Splash, Splosh	K Axon	46
Brother And Me	Carly Henderson	47
Young And Foolish	Pamela Blackburn	48
Childhood Dream	B M Martin	49
Young And Foolish	E Preece	50
When I Grew-Up	Pauline Matthews	51
The Concert	Rosemary Jennings	52
Listen And Learn	Hal Takata	53
The Kiss	Kevin Worsnop	54
One Day	Jane Jessop	55
To Be Young And Foolish	G Parker	56
The Philosophy Tree	Richard Lee North	57
Bull In A China Shop	Kim Rands	58
Safety First	Elspeth Law	59
Happy Christmases Past	Velma Winstanley	60
Young And Foolish	Margaret Dorothy Davies	61
The Girl I Was	Elizabeth Bernard	62
Young Dreams	Gladys McFall	63
Living Memories	M Kennedy	64
The Prize	Donald W Falconer	65
Yes! I Was Young Once	Alan Pollard	66
Memories Of Our Town Clock	Robert W Moore	67
Home Time	Anne Hadley	68
Perceptions Of Youth	Teresa Booth	69
School Kids	Carey Whitehead	70
Epitaph - Baby!	Peter J Moore	71
Child	Alison Glithro	72
Travelling Companion	Ann Stewart	73

Young And Foolish	Muriel Hughes	74
On Being Young	Edna M Sarsfield	75
Things Don't Change	Mike Orr	76
Staying Young	Margaret Sage	77
Teenage Talent : Triumphant	Richard Flemington	78
Teenage Tragedies	Maggie Smith	79
Visions Of The Past	Kate Brown	80
Love	Patricia Flynn	81
Childhood Self	J E Alban	82
Fateful Day Remembered	David Pearson	83
Emigrating!	Hilary Jill Robson	84
Untitled	Eilidh McMillan	85
Memories	Kristen Furley	86
When I Was Young	Maryann Foster	87
To Be Young	Lonwy Jones	88
Puppy Love	Dennis N Davies	89
The Best Days	Rachel Jones	90
We Were Only Eight	Frederick Seymour	91
Words	Evelyn Leite	92

FULL CIRCLE

I can remember being very small, perhaps only two or three,
And getting lots of petting on my mother's knee.
That time was very cosy, everything secure,
Worry was unheard of, life seemed very pure.
Then suddenly it was school time, the teachers rather stern,
The other girls weren't always kind, knocks we had to learn.
But learn we did the hard way, and schooldays were soon over,
We thought that working in the mill would be a bed of clover.
But up at six and off to work for a twelve hour day
Wasn't very thrilling for very little pay.
So better get a boyfriend and get married very young,
That could be the answer and obviously more fun.
Well, honeymoons don't last for long and babies soon appear,
They bring with them the heartache even though they're dear.
And as we nurse our daughters in our rocking chair,
We wonder if they'll take advice or will they just not care?
Will they make mistakes that we made or will they get it right,
Will everything repeat itself before they see the light?
Well now we've gone full circle, my child is on my knee,
What oh what will come to pass before she's old as me?

Patricia Battye

1973

Being told, when you are young,
How could you listen.
With summer nights so long,
... too busy to notice,
What's really going on.
Someone's calling your name,
But you're busy . . . it's nice in the rain,
And . . .
Remember, when you stole 'Bel Air',
From the lady in the greenhouse,
With the long blonde hair,
... Then we would hide . . .
Laughing, joking and smoking.
Then someone calls your name,
But, it's nice in your 'tank top',
Out in the rain . . .
... Then tomorrow,
We could do it again.

Tracie Mark Deakin

SPECIAL THOUGHTS

My grandad was a special man
Remember him? Of course I can
All things he did for me
Right from me being three
He used to take me walks for miles
It was always fun and full of smiles
Even when it was rainy or foggy
I'd go with grandad the pit moggy
We'd collect chestnuts from the wood
And look for mushrooms, that was good
We'd play for hours with his dog on the lawn
Then plant things in the garden until I'd yawn
He'd let me watch telly until time for bed
Then 'Goodnight funny face' he always said
He'd make me bubble blowers out of old wire
I'd watch my bubbles float higher and higher
My grandma was very special too
Not many things she couldn't do
She'd bake fresh bread all day long
Tell me a poem or sing me a song
I'd watched the dough rise on the fireplace
Even better, eating the bread, now that was ace
She'd hide my dummy in a place somewhere
Me and mum looked, but never looked there
Grandma said 'On the fire where they'll burn
You don't need dummies, that's the way to learn.'
But two special things they gave me before they passed away,
And I still cherish and have them even now today
And they're these lovely memories and my mother
They are the important things more than any other.

Tara Kay

NOSY PARKER

'You silly boy, you foolish child!'
He always drove the teachers wild.
He wouldn't read, he couldn't write
and stayed out questing day and night.
His aim, to know the birds and bees,
the grasses, flowers, shrubs and trees.
He pressed their blossoms, leaves and fronds,
caught sticklebacks and frogs from ponds.
Ignoring parents, whom he'd peeve
with muddied shoes and tattered sleeve.
On one occasion, tried to fly
from bedroom window through the sky.

With broken ankles, well again
he chose to make a secret den.
Within, he built and lit a fire
and sparked the hedge into a pyre.
The neighbouring bantams in their coop
found they were truly 'in the soup',
though fire-brigade and rozzers came
and Borstal finalized his game.

Poor 'Nosy' was no criminal
in fact his work proved seminal.
Eventually he passed the test
and joined society like the rest.
You'll find him, every single day
making a point, having his say;
still bent upon a lifetime mission,
now working for the Forestry Commission!

Ian T Colley

RECYCLED PAIN

My social worker called today,
She's actually, I suppose, OK.
I know I need help doing things their way,
But I don't understand what she's trying to say.
They'll come and take my kids one day,
And that's the price we'll have to pay,
For the sins of my parents.

In care I was since two or three,
My parents didn't try to see,
My brothers or sisters or me.
I struggled with identity,
I remember how I longed to be,
More than a distant memory,
To my absent parents.

They couldn't help, I know that now,
But still it doesn't help somehow,
To ease the pain or stop the rows,
The fear of separation grows,
My lack of understanding shows,
In all my heartfelt, desperate vows,
To be a better parent.

Beverley Christian

ANAESTHESIA

Objects slowly slide from my vision,
All sights are dulled,
All sounds are lulled,
So warm and soft,
Like floating aloft,
Now, I can't breathe,
Reluctant to leave,
I grasp a hand tight,
I feel I must fight,
No use, I am cast
Down, falling fast,
I call out in fear,
But, no-one can hear,
I'm lost, but O where?
I cry in despair.

How came I here?
No-one is near,
So I will wander
Through portals yonder,
Portals so high
They reach to the sky,
Inside it is cool,
Just like a pool,
With beautiful rooms
Of scented perfumes,
And spacious halls
But, nobody calls,
Strange music I hear,
Enchantingly clear,
Slowly creating
In me a longing,
A longing of what?
Ahh! I know not.

Now all is fading,
Music and longing,
Portals and perfumes,
All disappearing.
Then, voices I hear
And, now I fear . . .
Nurse, come here quick
I'm going to be sick!

G Richardson

DAYS GONE BY

The early start
The cold and the mist
The watching and waiting
The hoping and praying
That maybe this will be the
Day for the big one
The open fire to brew the tea
The sandwiches in little packs
But still the watching and waiting
And then a strike and the
Thrill of the pull on the line
Oh those days were great
Funny hobby for a girl
A lot of people said
But now it's not quite the same
Gone are the open fires
Gone are the sandwiches in packs
It's picnic or barbecue now
But still the watching and waiting
Still the thrill of the strike
And the pull on the line
Still people think, strange hobby for a woman
But it will never be the same
As those days gone by
Never to return
Fishing with my dad.

Rose Schwarz

The Dance Of Life

Two young people, girl and boy,
Dancing, leaping, full of joy.
The flashing lights of the disco hall,
Answering the drumbeat call,
Leap and dance for all to see,
You are beautiful, young and free.
Dance, dance, while you may
Tomorrow . . . is another day.
The tempo slows, the music calms
And lovers dance in each other's arms.
The young ones now, look for romance,
And there is nothing, nothing like the dance.
Soft lights on the ballroom floor,
Hearts beat together, wanting more.
Dance, dance, while you may,
Tomorrow . . . is a busy day.
The music fades, no time to dance,
Whatever happened to romance?
The fun and joy of youth is gone,
No longer dancing a happy song.
For the lessons of life, one has to pay,
Too soon tomorrow . . . becomes today.
Too late, too late, we learn the score
When we can leap and dance no more,
Just to join that happy throng
Leaping to the drumbeat song.
Alas! To have to keep one's seat
And be content to tap our feet.

V B Aspinall

MY DAD

At breakfast,
I was the child
caught up in his arms,
of the man in the cap
who'd been milking the cows.

In wind, rain and sun
he wore his flat cap,
lifting the brim
with his hard-working hands,
to ease the sweat on his brow.

Dorothy Fisher

TO BE YOUNG AND FOOLISH

'To be or not to be, I am going to do the same
For who is to stop me to be ardent lover?
I have no strings to be attached to my shame,
Nor I afraid to sunbathe in the clover!
I would strip myself below my waist
And roll my shorts to the higher hips
So that the sun would penetrate at last
Into my whole body, to make tingle with happiness my lips.
To be young and foolish? Who is to propose
These strange words to my personal appeal?
For not Adam and Eve rubbing their noses
Still being naked, with apple for their meal?'

Stanislaw Paul Dabrowski-Oakland

OUR CLASS OF 1952

In the year of our Lord nineteen fifty-two
Netball pigtails and pants shocking blue
Outside toilets all falling down
This was our school just outside the town

Chanting times tables by the glow of a fire
Old oaken desks with inkwells and carvings
Bright coloured marbles bought for penny three farthings
Steam train in the station the pulse of the nation

The sound of the whistle the swish of the cane
Prayers in assembly and songs in the rain
Trips to the theatre by charabanc
Chatter and squeals on the way home

Football with other schools on foreign pitches
A bucket of water to wash off the mud
Cigarette cards and conkers and milk tops to swap
The pride of the form when you came out on top

The smell of school dinners which drifted afar
The gristle the prunes and the rotten green veg
Standing in queues in a playground cold
Innocents awaiting a life to unfold

The long walk to school in all the seasons
Life seemed endless we asked no reasons
Pea souper fogs gas lamps like ghosts
The only way home was to follow the posts

Jam jars for charity the knock on the door
Bob-a-Job week but never a bore
Rich and poor pupils all pressed together
But all intermingling whatever the weather

Fifty-two pupils sat in the class
And in '52 triumph we all were to pass

M C Davies

OUR HEARTBEAT

Your *heartbeat* drives my heartbeat,
It keeps me alive, keeps in time with mine;
Your *heartbeat* beats for me,
It beats so we both can breathe.

My *heartbeat* drives your heartbeat,
It keeps you alive, keeps the beats in time;
My *heart* beats for you,
It beats as one person, contracts as one organ,
Never to be broken, or split in two;

And if this ever became so,

Then:
Your *heart,* my *heart,* would not drive each other,
Would no longer keep us alive,
They would stop beating in time;

And:
Your *heart,* my *heart,* would not beat for each other,
They would no longer keep us breathing,
Would no longer beat as one person, one contracting organ;

Just broken and split.

Dark Rose

EASTER MONDAY

My friend whose motorbike accident brought
him close to death for five minutes
has tasted another dimension where the
disabled and diseased are unshackled and alive.
The angels have heard my pleas.
He has been born again, given a means to
breathe, to live life anew.

I was clinically dead for five minutes after my
motorbike accident.
I tasted another dimension where the disabled
and diseased are unshackled and alive.
Things listen to my pleas.
I have been born again, given a means to shuffle
life anew.

Barry Welburn

TIME

Brief moments of silence
Time to reflect
On dreams that I had
And things I regret
So long ago
Since the world was mine
A lifetime ahead
My only enemy, time
Things could have been better
Things could have been worse
But once done, they are done
Time is a curse
A child has no fear
Of the future or past
It simply lives life
And presumes it will last
Then all at once
You suddenly know
Time is a river
And life is its flow
It carries you forward
You can never return
Just your mind to remember
And your heart to yearn
So my mind and my heart
Keep the memories real
But soon time will win
And my life it will steal

Julie Coulborn

YOUNG & FOOLISH

Young and foolish they said we were
And that it wouldn't last
For I had only just left school
And your first exams had passed
But as we were both in love
We couldn't really see
But went ahead without a care
For it seemed just you and me
We grew together you and I
We had our laughs and then we'd cry
And faced the world hand in hand
It always felt so very grand
But now alone I stand and wait
To meet you at the Pearly Gate
As our 40 years just flew by
Always together you and I
I never thought we would have to part
So when you went you took my heart
But we were blessed with three great sons
And grand-daughters now are our number one
The only thing that's foolish now
I have to carry on somehow
Without your loving face and smile
I'll try and stay just for a while
But young we will always be
And in my heart it's you and me
So I will never forget the day
We were young and foolish
For that's how we'll stay.

Joyce E Williams

SWEET REIGATE

These are the lips
of a girl that you kissed,
Who once loved you dearly
and hoped to be missed.

The trees at sweet Reigate
were confidantes true,
Boughs ne'er betrayed secrets
they heard - told to you.

And when, getting late
so many clocks chimed,
Their sounds covered distance -
the silence was kind.

Somehow we drifted,
with paths wid'ning out,
We'd had much in common,
and that's without doubt.

So often I drift
in my thoughts quite a while,
And think of sweet Reigate,
but now - it's to smile.

Frederica Morgan

Looking Back

My mind turns back the pages
To a time when we were young
We really were only kids and
Our lives had just begun.
You were so handsome with
Flashing blue eyes, just one look
could mesmerise.
I was thirteen and I was smitten,
And on my hand you had clearly written
your name, George Reed.
You told me that you loved me,
And I shyly said I loved you.
Little did you know that this would
be always and forever true.
And though our love lasted
for quite some time,
I knew in my heart that you would
never be mine.
We were to part through the jealousy
of your friend, but to me it was
a love that was to have no end.
And even now as I approach sixty
and have fully lived my life,
I wonder what you are doing
and who you took to be your wife.
But the innocent love that we shared
So poignantly pure and true
is still cherished deep within me
with yesterday and you.

Jean Kennedy

YOUNG AND FOOLISH

Foolish and young, that was never me
Giddy and feckless I was never to be
Was it me on that bicycle trying to race
With legs weak and trembling in vain to keep pace
With that spotty-necked boy with beloved red face,
To be held to ridicule reduced to hot tears
By the scorn of a man of seventeen years,
No that wasn't me I was surely too proud
To hug a damp pillow and murmur out loud
The name that I loved above all
The name that I now can hardly recall
When war came it found me still very young
Plenty to laugh at, silly songs to be sung
There were dances and socials, and men to be found
Who wanted to flirt and forget the dull sound
Of duty that called them from their own kith and kin
To laugh and to joke with, that's never a sin
It was then that I met him, my own precious dear
I wore his gold ring by the end of that year
My youth it died with him and is under that sea
So young, and so foolish. Ah yes! That was me.

Gladys Lamb

LIFE'S SPRINGTIME

Life's springtime dawns in innocence.
No cloud its sky of promise fills.
No anxious thoughts of morrow mar
The magic of today that thrills.
No sad regrets for yesterday
Disturb, for cares are quelled in rest.
Sweet pleasures grace each passing day -
With sheer enchantment life is blessed.

The butterfly in chrysalis
Knows not its future lovely form.
The dewdrop nestling in a flower
Knows not the fury of a storm.
The rose with petals tight in bud
Knows not 'twill ope to beauty rare.
The incubating egg knows not
'Twill hatch - a bird, to wing the air.

Likewise, the child at play knows not
What fate the future holds in store.
Play on, dear child! Your halcyon days
Will all too soon be spent and o'er.
Yet knowledge and experience gained
In tender, formative young years,
Will pave your path of destiny,
Which from life's waning spring appears.

Eileen N Blackmore

FEAR

As I sat at my window
The beauty around me drifted into sleep.
I sat there all alone
With fears pounding against me.
I was calmed by the soft breeze
That blew across my face
And the smell of the air that was coming at me.
I sank slowly into my chair
And thought about the things around me.
I closed my eyes but it was no good,
I needed country life
With the smell of fresh flowers
And the beautiful scenery.
I looked at the pictures around me
And wished I was there.

K V Land (12)

The Awakening

Leaves fall, tears fall,
And autumn settles slowly on my life,
We walked this path in blistering heat,
Where pebbles probed our naked feet,
And in those days of love, who thought of strife?

Blonde silk, tangled curls,
Two heads with minds so close entwined,
We danced the waves of summer seas,
Raining kisses in the breeze,
And chasing clouds of happiness, we left all woe behind.

Red sun, raw heat,
On screaming, throbbing wheels of silver flame,
We raced the ribbon of melting tar,
A glimmering, shimmering shooting star,
And in our reckless flight gave fear no name.

Silent dusk, secret dreams,
Where dormant feelings waken at a touch,
We soared through stars in indigo skies,
Heavenward bound on whispered sighs,
And knew then in our hearts we cared too much.

Cold wind, steel sky,
Around each corner sorrow lies in wait,
We watched our dazzling hopes take flight,
And bathe us in eternal night,
Now separately we dare the hand of fate.

Katy Melia

WISE WORDS

*Oogey-woogy doobledy-doodsy,
Woopsie-whoopie phrrr . . .*

These were the first words,
That my grandson said to me.

And,
I couldn't disagree . . .

I've often said the same thing myself.
Mostly to traffic wardens . . .

And others who seem to need,
Instructing in politeness

*Gurgy-wurgy oooooocacadoody,
Dumby-doodle phrrrrrr phrrrrrr,*

'I belong to the School of,
Don't-give-'em-time-to-think-Poetry'

Is that what he was trying to say?

Steve Taylor

MUM AND DAD

Mum and dad you mean a lot to me
You kept me fed, washed and clean
I know at times a word mis-said
Often got me sent to bed

When I was small I thought mum was cruel
Slapped on the legs for acting a fool
Clipped round the ears for starting a fight
Sent in the corner, it served me right

Dad, I remember, when I was young
Doing the house was so much fun
Stripping off walls or carrying blocks
A bag of goodies and a bottle of pop

Through bad times or good times you're always there
To help us get through and never despair
Mum and dad I love you both
This poem is from the heart where it counts the most

My problems and worries I've wanted to share
But I always thought you wouldn't care
I know you both do, in your funny ways
But it would be nice, for your views to say

I know you must think us girls are trouble
But what I would like is a parently cuddle
I wish we could talk open and free
Then there would be no reason to disagree

All I want to really say
I love you both more, each day
Mum and dad I hope you like this
I'll end it now with a daughter's kiss.

P A Deakin

A Memoir From A Budding Fag-Ash Lil

When I was a child in fifty-four,
I walked a quarter mile each morning for fags.
In rain, frost and snow. I hated this chore.
I didn't need exercise. It was a hell of a drag.

Both father and mother chuffed happily away
But when mom had no money or cigarette
It was best to be well out of the way
As I was usually in the front of anger beset

Only to expel the craving of old man nicotine
Then one morning to my dismay
No money, no fags, I hoped not to be seen
But my father had his final ace to play

Furtively gathered each nub end with no spat
The last cigarette paper gently smoothed open
Tobacco gleaned carefully and for what?
As it lay in the paper, this is true I am not joking

My mother coughed. Blew the lot into dust
Father exploded, tore his hair out bit by bit
After all their care, they felt it so unjust
Especially when I convulsed into a laughing fit.

J Baker

MY NIGHT OF REBELLION

'Mum, Dad can I stay at my friend's overnight to go to a dance?'
'You're not staying at your friend's all night there really is no chance.'
How unfair goes through my head I felt thwarted so annoyed.
I told my friend, she was so disappointed far from overjoyed.
Well decision made, that night after work at age of seventeen.
I did stay at my friend's house after going to dance
But peace of mind I never had, felt very unlike a queen.
My conscience would give me no rest
What a foolish thing I was doing to Mum and Dad at home, I felt nervous, apprehensive,
In morning I would have to face music, I was on my own.
Morning came, in great anxiety, home I went, I was grounded for
a week.
But to cause worry on score I did for my pleasure, to enjoy myself was
a disaster,
My fears I could not defeat, I never did anything like this again.
Young, stupid causing so much trouble never my aim.

Victoria Joan Theedam

FUNNY DAY

Oh, when I was little, I had this funny day,
I made-up a game, I played in such a funny way.
I jumped off the settee and landed on my bum,
I ran into the kitchen and flew into my mum.
She shouted at me and sent me off to my bed.
I did another mighty jump and landed on my head,
I looked in the mirror, on my head a glowing red lump.
I showed my mum, she said 'You must have had a nasty bump'
Tomorrow I'm going to be a bridesmaid for my Auntie Pat,
And now she's going to make me wear a hat.
I hate them silly, nasty things,
I'd rather wear some stupid fairy wings!
What shall I do, I shouldn't have been silly,
Now I've got to wear a hat . . .
. . . for the wedding of Auntie Pat and uncle Billy.

Hannah Jackson (10)

THEN AND NOW

I knew it all when I was small - and told my mother so -
and how she smiled.
Then when I was a WAAF - Oh! What a laugh,
I gave out orders everywhere,
To other WAAF's - that riled.

Then marriage - not quite as young as some,
I tried not to show
I knew it all, because no-one wanted to know.

Motherhood and blessings, - had to buy a book,
I didn't know a thing, but mother did,
So thanks to her, the baby,
soon had a bonny look.

The circle is completing now, I don't know anything,
I'm being told by someone young,
Computers are *the thing.*
The baby - now grown-up, is showing me the way,
I knew it all when I was small,
But I'm very dim today.

Vera Homer

MEMORIES

When I sit alone in the evening
And think of days gone by,
The happy days of childhood
That made me laugh - and cry.

Such carefree days they were to me,
They were for most of us,
We had so little to spend on fun,
But we didn't care, not us.

We'd pretend to be doctors and nurses,
Or teachers, or mothers with babes,
We imagined all sorts of things
There, in the good old days.

Then when we grew-up, all the dreaming
Became real, not play any more,
The boys became men, and fought for us
In war, real heroes for sure.

Now life has gone by, and we ponder
How lucky we have been,
With our loved ones to cheer us, and friends ever near us,
And memories for ever, to glean.

Ethel Grange

EDEN
(For Clair)

We grew together, like coffee-cherries
On Blue Mountain farms,
We were carried down
To Kingston town
In Lucy's strong, dark arms;
You were just a baby,
I was scarcely one;
But I remember Kingston,
And Lucy
And the sun.
The sapphire Caribbean
Hushed our infant cries;
We learned to walk,
We learned to talk
Under Calypso skies.
You were two
And I was three,
And life was scarce begun . . .
We sailed away from Kingston,
From Lucy
And the sun.

Eileen Pennell

FULL-UP

Whenever Patrick's tum felt needy
The lad was terribly, terribly greedy.
He ate and ate, and would not stop
We warned, 'Some day your tum will pop!'
One day ice cream was set for tea.
His eyes grew bright, he beamed with glee.
The rest were nibbling, so polite
While Patrick gobbled with delight.
His cheeks were bulging, eyes were popping,
But Patrick did not dream of stopping!
His tummy swelled with sickly stuff.
We really thought he'd had enough!
Quite suddenly the lad turned white,
Then red, then blue - he shook with fright.
With loud report he popped and burst -
(I said I always feared the worst!)
Within a second of a flash
He turned into an ice cream splash!
We watched with horror and with feeling
As bits of him shot to the ceiling.
The moral of this tale is sad
And must be heeded by many a lad.
That if you want to stay complete
Please don't take far too much to eat!

Pam Phillips

OBSERVATIONS AND EXAMPLES

'Have you ever been young Dad
Have you ever had fun
Have you always been old Dad?'
Enquired his little son.
'I got into mischief as you do son,
But it doesn't seem funny now
To knock on people's doors and run!'
His father replied with a frown.
'I frightened the life out of my Mum
With a spider on her pillow
I suppose I thought that that was fun
As I cleaned Dad's pipe with a 'Brillo.'
Soft soap in a ball with a sugary base
And giving it to a friend
Who spat it out and called me a name
And enmity now never ends.
Think hard, think long, and very deep
On harmful habits contemplate,
Just think my son before you leap,
For it is then too late!
Don't sit in the sun without a cream,
Or hack at the chairs with a knife,
Always cherish love's young dream,
Live a happy and healthy life.'

A J Ogg

MOTHER'S MILK

When I was born, you
Suckled me at your breast,
Instinct ruling where knowledge
Played truant.

At my weaning you chewed
For me, war making baby
Food a luxury you
Couldn't afford.

One frosty morning, I helped you
Bring in our ration of milk. The
Bottle, slipping through tiny
Mittened hands,

Smashed, covering the
Doorstep with a white,
Shimmering pool of your
Spilt love.

Peter Lee

To Be Young And Foolish

To be young and foolish they do say
But those were games of youth on those days
But sometimes then you go too far
You repeat the errors of your ways
Be young by all means but foolish no
Just take heed never let go
Fools tread where angels fear to walk
This we have learned and sometimes said
By those who have had their foolish games
Not caring who is holding the reigns
Youth is so beautiful so divine
But things never to as you planned
When you are young there are lessons to learn
But if you show you care - then (..no-one gets hurt..??)
As you grow older in your mellowed years
You look back at the foolish with a few tears
Live like grown-ups never be weak
For there's memories to treasure and to seek
Oh to be foolish oh to be young at heart
You had made your mistake right from the start
It started so innocent then ended in a lark
Then you knew you had been dropped in the cart
You always dreamed you would never part
But to be young and foolish is a broken heart.

N Tomlinson

My Fairies

When I was young, my fairies, would visit me each night,
And guard, and tell me stories, until the bright daylight,
And underneath my pillow, a tooth hid out of sight,
The tooth fairy would change it, for a new one, 'shining bright'
They used to leave me warnings, of trouble or bad news,
And fill the lawn with toadstools, if there was a chance I'd lose,
But if the news was 'happy', they'd leave a tiny bunch,
Of pretty little flowers, on top my rabbit hutch,
But when my schooldays started, and education ruled,
One by one, my fairies left, they knew I wasn't fooled,
For I was such a clever chap, I knew it all it seems,
And things like wands, and stardust, were no part of my dreams,
Now looking back, at my young days, before it all went wrong,
A happy little chap I was, with my secret magic songs,
Well now I take a 'factual' view, I know that I'm not nice,
See everything as black or white, with a heart that's turned to ice,
Lost, in this concrete jungle, wherever have I gone.
What I would give to hear again, those little fairy songs,
And run across the thistle field, to where the woods extend,
Racing 'elves' and 'pixies', to where the rainbow ends,
But fairy queens and grottoes, and super-fine stardust,
And granting all your wishes, all depend on trust,
But here with stress and finance, and people armed with guns
You bolt the door and 'look out', and learn to trust no-one,
I know if 'Puck', or 'Oberon', would visit me again
They'd mark my lottery numbers. 'But look at me in pain'.

Charles H Boyett

THE SKATEBOARD

The kids can do it, if I just wait,
I'll get a go upon their skate,
with helmet on, and knee-pads too
they show me, slowly, what to do,
then off I go, I'm on my own
looking like a Star Trek drone,
the kids all cheer and then they laugh,
I'm laying prone upon the path.

Anita Jane Smith

EXAM RESULTS

We all decided on the last day of school,
That summer would be a blast,
We'd do all the partying,
Before finding out if we'd passed,
The day was looming nearer,
My stomach was in knots,
I panicked non-stop,
Thinking of grades I might have got,
The day arrived; the postie didn't,
He came rather late,
He handed me the envelope,
And I passed all eight!

Kimberley Forsyth (16)

FRIGHTENING ENLIGHTENING

'Spare the rod and spoil the child'
That is why I was so wild,
The power of courts to cramp my style
Had been usurped for quite awhile.

My single parent wasn't there
So they took me into care.
No obstacles were put my way
So I stole by night and day.

Then I took to smoking pot
Paid for with the cash I'd got.
Soon this led to harder stuff
Of which I couldn't get enough.

More serious crime to feed my habit
Made me feel, a frightened rabbit.
How relieved when I was caught
Pushing grams of crack I'd bought.

On remand, I wish I'd died
'Cold turkey' really crucified.
After that, I'm going straight
A repeat I couldn't contemplate.

If only Dad had stayed with Mum,
How different life would have become.
If teachers could have used the cane
And discipline allowed free rein.

If policemen could have cuffed a yob
Instead of fearing for their job.
If the wretched system hadn't failed
No-one need have seen me gaoled.

Gordon Haines

ADOLESCENT FOLLY

Happy times when we were young, no stress or pain to mar the fun;
When every day was made for play, smiles of expectation all the way.
Favourite teddies hugged to death, then discarded for a newer toy,
Aunties calling in for tea, showering gifts galore,
Chocolate cake and cream with jelly,
Wide-eyed children filling tummies with delight;
Long hot summers on the beach, building castles in the air,
Watching waves creep in and wash them away without a
second thought.
Imagination ever near, fairies, magic never far,
Santa Claus, and the Easter Bunny, waiting to show their wares,
Excited faces, full of glee, as gifts appeared around the tree;
Then Easter Eggs for all to see.
Walt Disney filled so many hours, simple tales of make-believe,
Happy endings all the time, holding back, what was to come;
Then the teenage years soon entered in, growing-up with painted faces
and fingernails,
Freaky fashions, rainbow hair, parading around without a care;
First loves, valentines, the smiles and tears,
Tomorrow never in the plan, todays and yesterdays were only known.
Grown-ups were from another planet, they never understood,
Always dictating about the do's and don'ts not knowing right
from wrong.
Then came the culture shock, the four-letter word *work* was released,
We have to work, to live, to exist, simply to survive;
Meeting new people, making new friends, in the hostile world
of reality;
Feeling the hurt of a broken affair, the rejection of redundancy,
Or the grief after losing a loved one, such is life, the treasured days
of childhood,
Gentle times of folly and precious fantasy, are the best years of
our lives;
When being young and foolish didn't really matter,
Because we were all protected by our simple *innocence.*

Amanda-Lea Manning

MEMORIES OF CHRISTMAS

Christmas as I remember as a child of three
Was putting candles on our pine Christmas tree
All the excitement in the weeks before
Listen - is that Santa at our bedroom door
Dad helped Mom with the Christmas pud
He brought me a coat with a black velvet hood

I can still smell the giant turkey cooking
Took a large bite when no-one was looking
Once I found a silver sixpence in my share of the Christmas pud
As by the black-leaded coal fire I stood
Woke up very early on Christmas morn
Knew it was the day baby Jesus was born
Gave my big sister Joyce a shout
Then made quite sure everyone else was up and about
Decided to check the end of my bed
And sitting quite happily was a big cuddly ted
Oh for those lovely days once more
But now sadly Christmas can be such a chore

K Hines

CHANGES IN FARMING

When I was a lad I tailed the lambs with hot irons from the wood fire,
The cows were milked with bucket and stool and tied-up with chains in the byre,

The hay was cut from the loose haystack, the thatch kept it all safe and sweet
With whetstone and hay knife you cut out a flap and carried out for cows
to eat.

The milk was collected in heavy old churns with little jokes written under the lid
If the milk went sour you got it all back, 'twas different when I was a kid.

Now milking is all done by machine, everything must be scrupulously clean
And bactoscan results come regularly, it's fine if you know what they mean,

The milk is collected by tanker and nothing must get in its way,
On some farms they only see it but once every other day,

Silage is the feed of the future, the cows seem to like it that way
But to me there's nothing as sweet as a bit of old meadow hay.

The tractors are roaring great monsters with stereo sets and computers as well
Maybe one day they'll have a built-in toilet and a microwave as well

The world is moving faster and old craftsmen fade away
But it was better when life went slower and you could pass the time of day

R J Moultan

WINTER WHEN...

Snow crunched under freezing feet,
The sky was filled with liquid light,
Muffled music drifted through the streets,
And scarves and gloves were dusted white.

We raced on sleds; and sticks and coal
Were arms and eyes of rounded men;
We laughed and cried, and went outside,
And skidded on the ice of winter when . . .

They closed the schools down, once or twice,
A whole day off, and that was nice -
I wrapped-up warm but still the ice
Got down my neck (and into The House)

Sliding back down memory lane,
I miss the clouds of your misty laughter,
And I wonder if it will be the same again,
Winter today, and winters after.

A Humphrey

NOT ROSY TINTS

When I was young
I could not see,
Thoughts of metal
Hooked round eye,
Of shimmer glimmer
Sniping me . . .
Avoiding four-eyed chants.

Yet I suffered
And I shank
At each decay
Of chalky text;
How did no-one notice
That I was blinder
Than a bat.

That I was blinder
Than a mole
Left me digging
For a hole;
I wormed out
Of so much good,
I feared to do a thing.

Now I sit here
Writing this
With rimless rings,
With eyeball hats,
Disguised by what's
An almost lie,
A near conviction,
Circumspect.

Graeme Vine

YOUNG AND FOOLISH

If only I could be
young and foolish one last time
going out to parties and
drinking lots of wine
I'd like to go out dancing
to a disco or a club
then I'd go for one last drink
to our local pub
now the regulars in there would
get a really nasty shock
when they looked-up and saw me
in a little see-through frock
the top part of this dress would
not be very high and
the mini-skirt would have a split
right up to the thigh
I'd really let it all hang-out
because it's just a dream
but in real life I'd never make it
as a drama queen.

Francine

A Forgotten Language

I'm a teacher, and my man and I speak the Queen's English, or so we thought,
But we've just been to Canada where not everyone we met was a Scot.
We had real language problems, for we had not realised, that in truth,
We used many of the colourful words and dialect phrases of our youth.
For instance, when we talked about carrying a piece to work every day,
Some thought it meant we packed a gun and were ready for the fray,
And when my man said that hot dogs gar'd him grue and he was scunnered,
We realised that in translation, one guid Scots word was worth a hundred,
For we could not find the words to say in English what we meant,
And things went from bad to worse with every other day we spent.
We talked to the weans, and asked them if they could stoat a ba',
Or play keepie uppie wi' a fitba' up against a wa',
We talked tae their mithers, and tellt them how tae mak' a tattie scone,
But I doubt there'll no' be mony o' them wha will pit the girdle on.
One enterprising cousin's wife thought we should mebbe write it doon.
A list, she meant, of everything we saw when we were oot aboot the toon.
So we tried very hard to mind the words oor grannies taught us in the past,
And when we started, my, the auld Scots words cam' thick and fast.
See, ower on the cooker there's a pingle, a pot for boiling milk,
And there's a pirn o' threid. Tae you, that's a bobbin full of sewing silk.
And faither's got the gully, yon big knife he's gaun tae use tae carve the roast.
And grannie's got the cauld. Michty, the pair sowel has an awfy hoast!
We wrote down lots of other words too numerous to mention in this verse,
But truth to tell, I think we only made the situation ten times worse.
So we gave it up, and decided that we should just let confusion reign,
But oh! We had such a lovely wander down our dialect's Memory Lane.

Elizabeth Rae

SPLISH, SPLASH, SPLOSH

Splish, splash, splosh.
Big puddles
On the ground.
Splash, splish, splosh.
Playing out
In the rain.
Splosh, splish, splash.
Stomping in
The puddles.
Splish, splosh, splash.
Kicking up
The water.
Splosh, splash, splish.
There's water
Everywhere!
Splash, splosh, splish.
Soaking wet
And happy.

K Axon

BROTHER AND ME

You stand on the hill
You're the king of the castle
And I stand beside you
Just as the terrible two.

You were always there
When I would trip and fall
To pull me up
And rise above it all

Missions and adventures to be the heroes
Mum's rug makes our desert island
Full with sharks that lurk beneath
Night falls, we hide from giants that want us to
brush our teeth

Gone are the days of mud pies and camp fires
Now wages, jobs, music and a set of tyres
But still we stand side by side
To guide each other through the rollercoaster ride

Carly Henderson

YOUNG AND FOOLISH

I'd love to be young and foolish again
Young and foolish, the two combined
Would make my day, just fine.
Teenage years were my best time
Never a minute to spare.
Carefree days without a care.

Days filled with pleasure
Dancing was my forte
I could do this all day.
Drama school I tried but alas
I'm afraid, it was out of my class.

Saying this it gave me grace, I think?
Next was the ice rink
I really tried to get this off the ground.
But even with my grace.
I fell flat on my face

Girl Guides, I tried so hard
With the best will, they tried
To instil, a get-tough course.
I ended up climbing a hill
Camping and survival, weren't my scene
The hill was the last straw.
I thought there might be more?

I'd say young and foolish, I've been a bit.
If I had a chance again
I'd change my direction in men
I'd choose men, who could
Dance like me.
Then together we'd be 'Young and Foolish'
In harmony!

Pamela Blackburn

CHILDHOOD DREAM

I dreamt I was in a sweet shop and everything in there was free.
There were shelves and shelves of goodies and every one was for me.
I smiled and smiled at my good fortune let loose with all kinds
of sweets.
I floated round this sweet shop where no-one else there meets
There were brightly coloured pink, red, white and blue
The freedom of my childhood seemed to be coming true.
I dreamt the dream so often I thought I could eat the sweets
In my dream-like sweet shop where no-one else there meets
But I awoke and realised that it was only a dream that I could
dream tomorrow night.
And no-one could steal that dream scene.

B M Martin

YOUNG AND FOOLISH

Bring back my youth to me wrapped in gold foil
So that I can carefully unfold it and not harm it.
Let it spring out at me once again and envelop me in careless
Rapture and joy,
In excitement and apprehension,
In wonder and expectation.
Let the sunlight of those days shine on me
And let me feel the warmth of is glow,
Let me indulge in the uncertain chase
Of young men of my dreams
Risking rejection and humiliation,
Or feeling the exhilaration of success.
Let me sing and dance along the lane with my friends
And swing from hanging branches
And use umbrella leaves in the rain,
Let me remember the silly ditties we composed
Which prompted so much laughter,
Let me not think of the future but only know
That these days will last forever
Let me laugh and cry to the music
On my record player and in my heart,
And then carefully re-wrap my precious gift of
Youth with all its foolishness in its unspoilt gold foil.

E Preece

WHEN I GREW-UP

I wanted to be a hairdresser cutting and curling hair
I loved the different colours, brown, auburn and fair

I wanted to be a farmer's wife feeding ducks and pigs on the farm
Giving orphan lambs their bottles of milk and holding them in my arms

I wanted to care for animals, the sad lonely sick and abused
To give love, good food and a warm bed to those so very badly ill-used

I wanted to be surfer and ride on a clean fast wave
Then to lie in the sun on a beautiful beach or explore a mysterious cave

I've surfed a few waves in a modest way,
I've even watched some dolphins at play

I've cared for baby birds who fell from their nest
I've fostered abandoned dogs and always did my best

I have kids of my own and six grandchildren too
When they all come to tea it's like being in a zoo

But I really can't grumble, who knows what's in store?
I'll tell you what happens when I've lived a bit more.

Pauline Matthews

THE CONCERT

Giggling together my sister and me squashed into the ladies both trying to see in one tiny mirror as we
painted our eyes till they were large and black. Back-combed our hair as high as it went and sprayed on the hairspray until we had emptied the can,
then we hitched up our skirts until our knickers did show.
Finally ready we caught the bus to get to the city in time for the show.
Our dad would have been furious, he'd have made such a fuss
he always snarled at the telly all through Top of the Pops. Jut look at those yobbos they should get decent jobs and while they are at it they should get their hair cut. What a racket they're making, I'm sure they are on drugs.
Make sure you girls don't fall for that type, I won't have flower-power brought here in this house.
Finally we were there dancing and screaming, the Stones in concert shaking and grooving and us actually there waving and singing.
Soon we were running to catch the last bus, we were combing and brushing flattening our hair.
We were rubbing and cleaning at our black-eyes and pulling down our skirts, looking such nice girls
Dad made us cocoa and then went to bed and remains none the wiser the past thirty years.

Rosemary Jennings

LISTEN AND LEARN

I have many regrets that I don't really need
All because, when I was young, I didn't take heed
Of the advice given to me by older folk
And treated their concern as just a joke

Now that I'm older and, perhaps, wiser
I consider myself as a 'youngster adviser'
With the realisation that all those years ago
When I should have listened, I didn't want to know

If only we kept the sense we had when we were born
We wouldn't treat our elders with so much scorn
As their intentions are only to help us through life
So that we can all live a good one without any strife

But human nature being what it is
Young people think we can't mind our own 'bizz'
When they are convinced they know better than us
Experience is something that they have yet to 'suss'

Hal Takata

THE KISS

    As hero and heroine
kissed, romantic tears fell but factual
    credits rolled; and outside, the
dripping heavens mocked, city lights slurred in

    the greasy roads, motorised
rubber squealed, a drunken couple quarrelled
    and the restless river flowed.
Nevertheless, for a certain other

    twosome, walking hand in hand,
across the bridge, stars shone and their personal
    Palace of Dreams remained undimmed.
He therefore did what he had never before

    dared to: he took her in his
arms and kissed her crimson lips. Clark Gable
    and Humphrey Bogart (to name
but two) would have been proud of him, just as

    Vivien Leigh and Lauren
Bacall would have been proud of her. Rodin,
    of course, would have cherished them
both. Oblivious, though, cosseted by

    the limelight of illogical
love, they just celebrated their union,
    eating ices in the freezing
cold, together defying the curtain of rain.

Kevin Worsnop

ONE DAY

At the age of eight
I received a trike
Though I'd patiently wait,
And one day have a bike,
As years went on
I'd ride on two wheels
The peddle type though,
In between meals
Though one day I knew
My dream would come true
Then Christmas did accent
And to my shock and surprise
My dream bike was my present.

Jane Jessop

TO BE YOUNG AND FOOLISH

To be young and foolish
Is a time for fantasy and fun.
You think you can walk faster
Than you can run.
You think you resemble a film star
Then remember who you really are.
You discover if you are shy or bold
And not doing most things you are told.
Those little mistakes you make
And wondering am I a fake?
The thrill of dressing for a dance
Hoping for a new romance.
With each new experience
You learn something new
Then when you're grown up
You have your own point of view.

G Parker

THE PHILOSOPHY TREE

I was quite a childish youth whom people believed to be uncouth,
until the day I met a tree, I swear, began to talk to me!
It's voice from outset craved attention as it spoke with strong conviction;
'I'm your tree of philosophy, pray, listen to my liturgy.'
The tree became my wise adviser, teacher, preacher, able master,
moralist, guru, even friend, its list of functions had no end.
And yet it was a jealous tree, always watching over me,
advising me against all pleasure, rest, enjoyment, times of leisure.
'Take a leaf from my good book,' it told me with a righteous look,
'Live a life of stoicism, stifle all emotionalism.
Do not shun this perfect code, it will protect you from the load
sin would impose in order to stop you rising above to realms so true.'

I met a girl about this time and fell in love, like poet with rhyme,
the tree observed me with disdain and said I'd gone against the grain.

This was the final straw for me and I prepared to face the tree
with axe in hand to cut it down, the king, he was to lose his crown.
It was a painful thing to do, for, as the blade cut through so true
the tree began to wail and cry, I thought that it would never die.
It lay there bleeding, softly pleading that I stay as it was needing
for to weakly talk to me before it was a lifeless tree.
Heavy guilt, a tear I felt as I prepared to pray, and knelt
before the tree that once meant all, I heard it crying through its call;
'Please tell me why this was to be, I loved you, did you fail to see
my lofty commands were all an act to save you from the devil's pact.'
'I'm sorry, tree,' I weakly said, thinking then that it was dead,
'I suppose I wasn't worthy enough to join you in your realms above.'
Surveying the scene a final time I dropped the axe that did the crime,
then I left the place alone to begin my troubled journey home.
I walked through wind and stinging rain (for winter had returned again),
I passed through many a shaded lea . . .
and a forest of trees I failed to see.

Richard Lee North

Bull In A China Shop

When a bull sees red,
Be it in a china shop or not,
Tension is broken,
The bull is seen in his true light,
As a mere calf.

Why the storage of so much emotion,
When the grass is greener for him now.

As he receives love,
He never feels its touch,
Being young and blinkered,
He only sees the green of envy,
The red of fear and anger,
Isolating himself.

Kim Rands

SAFETY FIRST

My sister Kath
and me
slept in the
pantry
which was under
the stairs
in the war

Safe from the
bombs
that dropped in
the night
on the mountains
around

But later
we found
the stairs
are the first
to crumble.

Elspeth Law

HAPPY CHRISTMASES PAST

We didn't have much money when we were small
Our parents couldn't afford much at all
The kids today want presents families can't afford
If they don't get what they want there's discord
A family we had you see
Meant a lot to my brother and me
Christmas tree nuts and mistletoe
Lovely fire a lovely warm glow
Toys we got though they were few
So we kept them like new
With people you love and love all around
Is the best Christmas to be found
Lovely memories like this don't fade away
My happiness of my childhood will always stay
Now Mum and Dad have gone alas
I'll always remember happiness of Christmases past.

Velma Winstanley

YOUNG AND FOOLISH

In middle years I thought
'Life's gone'
But then I heard that
awesome song
'Fools rush in where angels fear
to tread'
and so I thought
I'm not quite dead.
Heartbeat quickened at some pace
now I'm with the human race.
Joined yoga, swimming and the squash
golly, gosh, all's not lost!
New hips in place
so can't be bad.
In middle years
I'm not too sad.

Margaret Dorothy Davies

THE GIRL I WAS

The years have gone by
And I'm still here
Waiting for a change
But,
Nothing's changed
It's all the same
Each day just filled with pain.

I let the pain come
And I just pray
And hope the praying works
But,
Every day comes, and every day goes
And still,
Everything hurts.

When I look around
And observe my life
I want to sit and cry
How did things turn out
This way for me?
And also,
I ask myself,
Why?

I really used to
Like my life
And now,
I can't believe
That each new day
Just brings more time
For me,
To mope and grieve.

Elizabeth Bernard

YOUNG DREAMS

I was looking for a rainbow
With its shiny pot of gold,
Hoping when I'd find it
I'd watch my dreams unfold.
But I was so enchanted,
It totally slipped my mind,
That what you're always looking for
Isn't always what you find.
Someone forgot to tell me
My search would be in vain,
Cos before there is a rainbow
There's always lots of rain.

Gladys McFall

LIVING MEMORIES

I remember my
Youthful
Activities.

Looking forward to the weekends,
With brass
Burning
Holes in pockets,
Itching to be spent.

Early evenings in the pubs
Drinking,
Late nights, at the clubs,
Dancing,
Forever performing
Mating rituals.

My
Energy,
Dreams, and
Optimism
Propelled me through
Life.

And now, at forty-five,
Nothing
Has
Changed,
I'm still 'young and foolish'!

M Kennedy

THE PRIZE

Out of the blue, burst a stream
of honeyed beams, melting buttercups on a hill.
In that light, we ventured to dream,
near a cliff edge, for the power of will.
Green grass twinkled and glistened
on that beauty spot, so we named
our prize, which lurked below, we listened
as the turquoise waves leapt and flamed
against red sandstone, thus sending
creamy spume to sail aloft in bubbles;
but still we gauged our quest, pending
courage, as the pearly eggs lay in huddles
below, abundant in their nests, while
angry gulls squawked their protection: Down
the face I watched him descend, tensile
tight for life. Each foothold a noun
in his life. Each hand seeking out
a verb. 'Got three,' I heard him cry:
I followed, my heart full of doubt.
Still, down I progressed, until there, just by
my shoe. I spied a nest. Suddenly!
I am attacked - my feet slip -
my fingers follow. I am lost to gravity.
Down, down, downwards. A hellish trip.
I whirled in a vortex with the dead.
Thud! I landed on a grassy shelf below,
just missing a large boulder with my head.
I broke my back, both legs and a toe.
Yet oddly they found, or so they said,
an egg nesting in my hand. 'Never,' I pleaded.

Donald W Falconer

YES! I WAS YOUNG ONCE

Today was an awakening
From the tears of my lonely eyes
Came the cries of childhood
A thousand years of dreaming
Could not change the times
As my world lay open to the forming visions
I am reliving again and again

The shifting sands of beachheads
The deepening sorrow of the heroes
This all a reality surviving in memories
A chasm of doubt resting upon minds and shoulders
Yet we never once questioned our orders
It's only now that I can.

Yes I was young once
Yet the years slowly slipping
Bring closer the voices of friends who had fallen
Edging further from sadness towards life again
It all lay forgotten and now it stands clear
My friends are alive in my memory's eyes
And I'm still alive in the world.

My tears make stars
Upon the blackness of the war
And year after year
We remember our fellow soldiers
It's such a pity we never saw
Our dreams come true
For our childhood lay too close
To history's darkest days.

Alan Pollard

MEMORIES OF OUR TOWN CLOCK

When I was just a boy it seemed,
That I would never know,
Whate'er it was made that old clock,
In our Clock Tower go.

I used to listen day by day,
Ear at the keyhole there,
'Twas just as if an old man swayed,
In his old rocking chair.

Click tick, click tock it sounded like,
Or something of that kind,
But then a rumbling mumbling came,
And it began to chime.

Then back again the same old sound,
Each minute of the day,
Like the rockers of his chair on ground,
As to and fro he'd sway.

But one day when I came to see,
I had the greatest shock,
The clocksmith with the metal key,
Was winding our old clock.

No rocking chair in there to sway,
No mystery no more,
Just wheels and chains going round all day,
Behind that old clock door.

Robert W Moore

HOME TIME

Amongst these hands and little faces,
Glows the love of God of ages,
See his hand has made these faces,
Given them no airs and graces,
Given them these little faces.
Angels of the classroom places,
Where their little hands explore.
'Please Miss, may I use the toilet,'
'Where is the way back home to Mum,'
'Can I go now Miss?'
'I've found it,'
'Now can I please go back home?'
'Miss I've looked here in the cupboard,'
'Miss I've really had enough,'
'Miss, can I read the story, I know all
That baby stuff.'
'Please, please Miss,
My teacher
Can I go back
Home
To Mum?'
'Surely, surely, I have learnt it all now
Teacher'
'Now it's time to suck my thumb.'

Anne Hadley

PERCEPTIONS OF YOUTH

Did I really grow up in the dark ages
As youngsters today would have me believe?
Laughing disbelievingly as they hear my story.
Oh the horror of no television, no piped images of colour
Oh the pleasure of those Thursday evenings past
Crowded into a friend's small front room
Outnumbering tolerant parents, weekly enduring our
'Top Of The Pops'
Silence prevailing as the huge reel to reel tape recorder
Captured our music, parental sighs and rustling newspapers.
Eager for the moment when speech and normality could return.
Oh the horror of no film of recorded visual images
To accompany the captured musical sound!
Difficult for them to comprehend the world of my youth
When children played and adults really talked.
When a country walk was considered a good day out.
When streets were safe and violence a rarity.
I hear stories told of the era of my youth
Thus I reflect and wonder, did I really miss out?
What really happened to the well publicised legend
Of the sixties, sex, drugs and rock and roll?
My own personal experience testifies to the myth.
Perhaps I am too young after all!

Teresa Booth

SCHOOL KIDS

Do you remember when we were kids
Had such fun playing in the rain and sun
In the school yard you'd pull her hair
Take a shilling for the dare
Swings and roundabouts, boats and trains
Dolls' houses, boys and girls playing games

Sitting in the classroom, gum in your hair
We'd get the stick if heard to swear
Dodging out of maths, capping off games
Down to the bridge spotting trains

Smoking in the toilets, they didn't catch me
Kissing with the girls in the library
Secret meetings behind bicycle sheds
Puppy love going to our heads
Remembering the days when we were free
All the boys and girls, you and me

We were school kids having fun
Just school kids out in the sun
Splashing in puddles, laughing in the rain
Wish those days were back again
Lost in innocence, life was fun
Never worried time was on the run
A little trip down memory lane
Yes I wish those days were back again.

Carey Whitehead

EPITAPH - BABY!

Do you remember, baby?
Under the yellow-green stain of electric light,
Bleeding like sudden wounds down smoke-dried walls,
And the jukebox blare over cameod laughter.
Jerk and pain -
Moving like greased bearings
Through ooze and scrape of spilled pale ale and dog-ends,
Meandering past iron-work table tops,
Eddying back along the eyeline
Of my returned stare.

And if by then, baby,
You saw the pain and blood through cider eyes,
You caressed the moment of my perfect vanity,
And danced upon the anguish of crumpled pride.
Hip and thigh -
Sliding through smoke
From spark and innocence, when I caught you up with kisses,
And sent you head-long into loins,
To the precise leer of your contempt
For my contemptible smile.

And now I am glad, baby,
That your dark blood eyes of imprecise vision
Did not see the mirror in my dull eyes,
That with sullen rage returned your gaze.
Skid and burn -
The tear of metal.
Too quick for tears as screams gurgle and drown in blood,
Sliding on the crest and fall of years,
Through hollow dark resounding eyes
Of my regretfulness.

Peter J Moore

CHILD

With every breath and beat
You sense and learn
Something new
With every turn
And from your mouth
Another word,
A different sound
We haven't heard
Before.
Then you crawl
To the door, locked tight
To keep you
Safe in sight.
Soon you begin
To toddle, stumble,
Run too soon
And take a tumble.
And so you
Reach out and cry
For mother who soothes
The teardrops dry.
Dream time, in your bed
Snuggled down deep
Small, sweet and innocent,
I watch you sleep
Knowing through your life
I will protect and guide,
Nurturing unconditional love
Between mother and child.

Alison Glithro

TRAVELLING COMPANION

He got on the train at Trew and Moy.
I ignored him
And went on enjoying my P G Wodehouse.

From time to time I was aware
That he was appreciating my enjoyment,
But I continued to ignore him.

At the GNR station in Belfast
He offered to carry my case.
My 'No thank you' was cold, distant, journey's end.

I never saw him again . . .
Yet something about the way his eager smile faded
Travels with me still.

Ann Stewart

YOUNG AND FOOLISH

Will he telephone, or won't he?
Will he look at me or not?
Will I like him quite as much
Or, will I like him, not one jot?

I'll follow him from place to place;
He'll come to me and say, 'Hello'
I'll memorise his handsome face:
To be ignored, oh! What a blow!

If pride be smashed to smithereens
What difference will it mean?
It's youthful foolishness to dream
Of all the things that might have been.

Muriel Hughes

ON BEING YOUNG

When I was young, and
foolish was my middle name
no matter what the reason
I played the blushing game

Caught out in a prank
egged on by those who knew
no matter what the reason
I retained their rosy hue

Introduction to a boy
held misery untold
no matter what the reason
my cheeks grew pink and glowed

My teenage years were purgatory
shedding many a tear
no matter what the reason
two bright spots would readily appear

Excited at the prospect of
attending my first dance
no matter what the reason
I would blush at every glance

Would I ever grow up
and quit the blushing game
no matter what the reason
would it always be the same

The only consolation of those
young and foolish years
is the very reason
this poetic verse appears.

Edna M Sarsfield

THINGS DON'T CHANGE

It's funny that as you get older,
You realise you know less and less.
At sixteen, I knew everything,
Although my mum always thought she knew best.

Clothing always caused aggravation,
My mum's attitude seemingly odd.
What's wrong with burgundy loon pants,
Pale blue silk jacket and clogs?

She always thought my friends were iffy,
Just because they'd spent time inside,
But it was cool to hang out with the heavies,
And she couldn't stop me, however she tried.

I hated being an apprentice,
My friends all earned more driving vans,
But now I'm much more successful,
So I'm glad I stuck with the plan.

So now, it's my turn to suffer,
And *my* kids are causing me grief.
They're convinced that I know nothing
But they'll learn, there's no doubt, wait and see.

Mike Orr

STAYING YOUNG

I used to love to play outside
When I was a little child.
Skipping ropes, marbles and outdoor games,
Trees we used for climbing frames,
Now it's all computer games.

Children, not many play in the street
With skipping ropes around their feet.
I don't remember all their names,
But in my mind I have them framed.

The village dance was once a week,
Looking back it was a treat.
Now the disco's here to stay
It's this generation's heyday.
What comes next the space shuffle hop
With silver pants and silver tops.

Going out is still good fun,
I try to stay rather young.
A disco now and then I go,
It's easy swaying to and fro.
The young ones keep me on my toes,
Advising on make-up and my clothes.

I won't give in or give up hope,
We are not here to sit and mope.
To see the young ones having fun,
Reminds me of when I was young.
For in my heart I will always be
A recycled teenager, happy and free.

Margaret Sage

TEENAGE TALENT : TRIUMPHANT

Life sometimes produces depression,
In my case replaced by elation;
For zooming on high, then subsiding,
Comes this burning desire for creation.

To produce a superlative: 'Something'.
Fired by this urge to create,
I will *act;* I won't let it grow fainter,
Towards: too late; too late, it's too *late!*

I've tried this and that,
On my face fallen flat,
As actor, pop singer and writer -
Then a brilliant thought strikes;
'A bolt from the blue'.
An idea so simple, inspiring
And true -
Its conception could never be brighter.

I'll sit down and relax,
Take a pen in my hand,
With the whole of my soul:
Boy - *I'll show 'em!*
Emerging with passion
From my artistic womb,
I'll give birth to -
A *world-shattering poem!*

Richard Flemington

TEENAGE TRAGEDIES

Black leather jackets
Dark blue jeans
Cigarette packets
Girlish screams.

Guttural voices
Growling bikes
Grinding noises -
Animal strikes!

Into first
Second
Third -
Thunder burst
Or maddened herd?

Fifty
Sixty
Eighty-one
Joyful yells -
Done a ton!

Burning,
Churning,
Turning -
Now!

Raging beast
Mighty master,
Engine ceased -
Cased in plaster!

Maggie Smith

VISIONS OF THE PAST

Great, you're sitting there one day, minding your own business,
Then suddenly - *bang!*
It wasn't the first, won't be the last
Oh yes! Visions of the past
When I was a youth I thought it was fun,
Running about sporting a gun
It was great to be in with the 'in-crowd'
Mouthing off, shooting off, very loud
Oh yes! Visions of the past.
A bomb was nothing, it could be built with speed
Laughing and joking, we paid no heed,
To the carnage that we wrought
Oh yes! Visions of the past.
Now age has set in, the bangs grow louder and louder
As my heartbeat grows faster and faster
No! It can't be, it can't be another disaster!
Where are my sons, my daughter, my wife
Are they out there, fighting for life?
While I sit here, head in hands
Oh yes! Visions of the past all too clear
I helped kill others for a stupid cause
My days are numbered, my shame is complete
It is my family dead on the *street!*

Kate Brown

LOVE

Love can be anything
From April showers
To early spring
Stately trees
Summer flowers
Love will do amazing things
Meander through woods
Colours of the earth
Spectrum of the rainbow
Cherubs at birth
Autumn colours
Behold our eyes
Frosty mornings
Winter skies
Bird on wing
My heart sings.

Patricia Flynn

CHILDHOOD SELF

Once upon a time I wished wishes
Dreamed dreams spun tales
With threads of my imagination
Creating silvered seas over which I'd sailed
Through rainbow skies of red and blue
Yellow moon kissed by shooting stars
As I'd be kissed by a prince
Who'd travelled to me from afar.
Happiness was all I'd dreamt;
A kind husband, a child or two
In a cottage with roses wild
Rambling around the door a few.
No clouds in my childhood sky -
Only rainbows and shooting stars.
But then, redundant was my father
For work, he moved afield far.
When next a roof I shared with him
He had changed, almost a stranger;
But I without knowing had changed too.
My childhood self was in danger,
For childhood had almost been
Left behind as I grew,
For almost a woman I was then -
My childhood self flew.

J E Alban

FATEFUL DAY REMEMBERED

I remember my childhood, I can visualise days
Where the sun burned for hours through an endless blue haze
I remember school football striped yellow and green
Running hard on the right wing with professional dreams

When I reached eleven, all the threads of youth parted
A chair on its side, Dad lay dead on the carpet
The yacht on the table held all my Dad's dreams
But his heart, like the sailcloth, tore apart at the seams

I remember a neighbour long thumping Dad's chest
I remember a dark van and the Chapel of Rest
I remember the coffin moving slowly on rails
A journey through curtains, like jaws of a jail

I remember the gardens where the ashes are scattered
We planted a tree there, only memories mattered
I remember that Christmas, I remember the gloom
I can still see my mum sat alone in that room

David Pearson

EMIGRATING!

Anxious about
Going to live in a strange land,
Foreign to us and pals, beforehand,
Learned about region second-hand
From others, to make us understand.

We were to live
With foster-folk, old, maybe young,
Another country, somewhere far-flung
And natives spoke in lilting tongue
Where English dwelt too, to be among.

'Live with natives!
Who wear grass-skirts? - 'Not that native!'
We're feeling pensive, apprehensive,
Parents being so persuasive
We three sat sullen and pervasive.

Prior had not
Strayed from home or neck of the woods,
Had lived in our house from babyhood.
Now into junior girlhood
Compelled to leave friends and neighbourhood.

We felt unwell,
Butterfly tummies and shaky,
Too sick to go, hot, headachy,
'You needn't start that *malarkey*
What I say goes in this monarchy!'

On arrival,
Tumbled from carriages like mail,
Saw the natives and turned deathly pale,
Miners blackened head to toenails,
Evacuation to foreign parts - Wales.

Hilary Jill Robson

UNTITLED

Ripped from my womb by a premature call.
Your promise of life gone in a hospital room.
Too young I told myself
to justify this murder,
too selfish, too scared,
now I know better.
For still I hear your silent crying
and I comfort you in my heart.
Rocking your cradle in a mind no longer mine,
given over to the memory of you
and of what might have been.
Rest easy child of mine for I have not forgotten.
Rest easy child of mine for I never will.

Eilidh McMillan

MEMORIES

Memories,
So many of them,
Each of them as clear as day.
But one particularly foolish time
Is just as bright as yesterday.

It was my first step into this crazy world in which we're to survive,
My first taste of the confusion and blindness I had stepped into.
This memory is as fresh as my laughter now,
But it was really very simple, when looking back on it.
I just didn't know how to reach out and grab hold of it,
But with practise I learned to control it.

I became its master,
For it to bow down to my knees and to obey me forever more.
I played and toyed with it,
Enjoying the freedom of power.
But things change,
And that day everything changed.

My eyes boiled hot as they laid sizzling on the new appearance
in my life,
My mouth went dry and suddenly I was a weak puppy once more,
Pathetic and alone.
I remember the first breath I took after that moment's awe,
And I choked myself in exaggerated slyness and confidence.
How I thought much of my superior attitude towards it,
And how it humiliated me!
I was crushed by my melted confidence and stinking embarrassment.
And all I had to do was to be myself and not the mask I had played.

How I laugh now at that foolish moment,
And the change that I overcame and under-came I now know well.
Very well,
Because I have been in love for almost my eternity.

Kristen Furley

WHEN I WAS YOUNG

When I was young I did not know
that famine took its toll
in far-off countries where the sun
dehydrates the soil.
I had not seen those skeletons,
those children without food,
whose bellies round
deceive the eye where flies
and sickness brood.

I sucked and played with cuddly toys
and cried for more, yet more,
but now those hollow faces lie
like shadows at my door.
'Why has she got food, not us?'
the begging hands strike home.
'Look at us, we're human too.
Give now, our bread is gone.

A seed is not a grain of sand
it multiplies until
the earth is green with ears of corn.
Hear us if you will:
without the rain our crops dry up
they wither on the stem
and if you do not share your food
then we shall die like them.'

Maryann Foster

TO BE YOUNG

The whole world was mine when I was young.
Adolescent years had just begun.
'If your urge to be foolish is so immense
Never forget your common sense.'
Wise words spoken by Mum and Dad
The best parents anyone had.
My great expectations were not to last
A deadly bacteria was chasing me fast.
Gruelling treatment and seven months ahead
I was ready to leave my hospital bed.
Up on my feet and struggling to walk,
Doing my best to listen and talk.
Five months later I was ready for home,
To gather memories and on hills to roam.
The hills I loved when I was a child,
Where with my family I ran so wild.
We chased the falling stars at night
By day rays of sun was our delight.
When sun and rain came down together
We walked under rainbows and thought we were clever.
I met my sweetheart when in my teens,
A new beginning to reality and dreams.
Wedding bells rang throughout the valley,
Two hearts jointed together, we were so happy.
Blessed with children, life was a song,
Through long happy years what could go wrong?
My loved one I lost but not forever,
Some day, we shall always be together.
His star shines down from Heaven above
Just to remind me we are still in love.

Lonwy Jones

Puppy Love

There's a puppy in our kennel
A lovely little chap.
Whenever, there's anyone about
He always starts to yap.
To draw their attention
That he wants to play.
A friendly little fellow
Though he has, a cheeky way.

Making sure he's noticed
Cos he is rather small
But they know, they are welcome
When he shares with them his ball.
He'll give a little bark
Roll over on the floor.
He loves a bit of fuss
As friends come through the door.

Out will come his toys
As fast as he can run.
As soon as he wakes up
He thinks it's time for fun.
Sometimes, he'll just curl up
Right between our feet.
It's since, we brought this puppy
Our lives seem more complete.

Dennis N Davies

THE BEST DAYS

Born on a gloomy Sunday night,
the misbegotten offspring of
militant ideals and
clammy hormones,
my adolescence grew.

From a vapid start
it aspired to right the world,
learn how to smoke,
and waive its virginity.

It gathered momentum quickly,
fumbling in the dark,
playing in a band,
all the time
working to its own secret objective.

When finally it expired,
it lay, like a deflated rubber,
unusable, beyond revival.

It bequeathed me things,
I still have them even now,
memories I can't erase
and half a dozen tattoos.

Rachel Jones

WE WERE ONLY EIGHT

From school.
We came home for dinner.
Crawford St School was nearby.
We had stew made with rabbit.
My pal Lennie and I.

The days were warm it was summer.
So before returning to school
we could play.
But the air-raid siren sounded
and stopped us playing that day.

I remember we stood in the passage
for safety.
My Mum Lennie and me.
We could hear the drone of the low
flying bomber.
'It will soon pass over,' said Mum
to Lennie and me.

The all-clear siren sounded.
It was late, but there was no missing school.
We climbed over bricks and debris.
Two boys aged eight, and so small.

Two eight-year-olds in school chatting.
'We got bombed,' we told all of our chums.
No trauma counselling in these times.
We were told to get on with our sums.

Frederick Seymour

Words

Three words on a grubby square of paper
hid by a child's hand, in a niche,
in a tree in the park, secretive,
a hint of the forbidden, not understood
but magically there, to blossom unaware
in later squares and longer words
more open, brazen, flauntingly 'don't care';
words in love with themselves, not experience,
letters to soothe a broken heart, to incite
or right a wrong, taunt, praise, question,
hint, forgive, such varied words
this hand has writ; when some did fall
on wrath, the price to pay was gross . . .
lives fell by the wayside, wordless
time consumed them, dressed them
in new meaning, so they live, scarred
perhaps enriched; words are wanton,
some may trace and penetrate, or not discern,
no lesson here to learn, just bare words,
a story written in life's blood
all because of words so loved, idealised,
meanings with no intent but to remain
beautifully crystallised through the years
in words and tears . . . and words
and words . . . and words.

Evelyn Leite

INFORMATION

We hope you have enjoyed reading this book - and that you will continue to enjoy it in the coming years.

If you like reading and writing poetry drop us a line, or give us a call, and we'll send you a free information pack.

Write to :-
**Triumph House Information
1-2 Wainman Road
Woodston
Peterborough
PE2 7BU
(01733) 230749**